HUMANITIES DEPARTMENT

ALSO BY LUCILLE CLIFTON
Good Times

GOOD NEWS
ABOUT THE EARTH

GOOD NEWS
ABOUT THE EARTH

new poems by LUCILLE CLIFTON

 RANDOM HOUSE, NEW YORK

for the dead
of Jackson and
Orangeburg
and so on and
so on and on

Contents

About the Earth

Heroes

Contents

Some Jesus

ABOUT THE EARTH

1

after Kent State

only to keep
his little fear
he kills his cities
and his trees
even his children   oh
people
white ways are
the way of death
come into the
Black
and live

2

being property once myself
I have a feeling for it,
that's why I can talk
about environment.
what wants to be a tree,
ought to be he can be it.
same thing for other things.
same thing for men.

3

The Way It Was

mornings
I got up early
greased my legs
straightened my hair and
walked quietly out
not touching

in the same place
the tree   the lot
the poolroom   Deacon Moore
everything was stayed

nothing changed
(nothing remained the same)
I walked out quietly
mornings
in the '40s
a nice girl
not touching
trying to be white

4

the lost baby poem

the time i dropped your almost body down
down to meet the waters under the city
and run one with the sewage to the sea
what did i know about waters rushing back
what did i know about drowning
or being drowned

you would have been born into winter
in the year of the disconnected gas
and no car   we would have made the thin
walk over Genesee hill into the Canada wind
to watch you slip like ice into strangers' hands
you would have fallen naked as snow into winter
if you were here i could tell you these
and some other things

if i am ever less than a mountain
for your definite brothers and sisters
let the rivers pour over my head
let the sea take me for a spiller
of seas   let black men call me stranger
always   for your never named sake

5

later i'll say
i spent my life
loving a great man

later
my life will accuse me
of various treasons

not black enough
too black
eyes closed when they should have been open
eyes open when they should have been closed

will accuse me for unborn babies
and dead trees

later
when i defend again and again
with this love
my life will keep silent
listening to
my body breaking

6

apology
(to the panthers)

i became a woman
during the old prayers
among the ones who wore
bleaching cream to bed
and all my lessons stayed

i was obedient
but brothers i thank you
for these mannish days

i remember again the wise one
old and telling of suicides
refusing to be slaves

i had forgotten and
brothers i thank you
i praise you
i grieve my whiteful ways

7

Lately
everybody I meet
is a poet.   "Look here"

said the tall delivery man
who is always drunk

                                    "whoever can do better
                                    ought to do it. Me,
                                    I'm 25 years old
                                    and all the white boys
                                    my age
                                    are younger than me."

So saying
he dropped a six pack
turned into most of my cousins
and left.

8

the '70s

will be the days
I go unchildrened
strange women will walk
out my door and in
hiding my daughters
holding my sons
leaving me nursing on my self
again
having lost some
begun much

9

listen children
keep this in the place
you have for keeping
always
keep it all ways

we have never hated black

listen
we have been ashamed
hopeless   tired   mad
but always
all ways
we loved us

we have always loved each other
children   all ways

pass it on

10

Driving through New England
by broken barns and pastures
i long for the rains of Wydah
and the gardens
ripe as history
oranges and citron
limefruit and African apple
not just this springtime and
these wheatfields
white poets call the past.

11

The News

everything changes   the old
songs click like light bulbs
going off   the faces
of men dying scar the air
the moon becomes the mountain
who would have thought
who would believe
dead things could stumble back
and kill us

12

the bodies broken on
the Trail of Tears
and the bodies melted
in Middle Passage
are married to rock and
ocean by now
and the mountains crumbling on
white men
the waters pulling white men down
sing for red dust and black clay
good news about the earth

13

Song

sons of slaves and
daughters of masters
all come up from the
ocean together

daughters of slaves and
sons of masters
all ride out on the
empty air

brides and hogs and dogs and babies
close their eyes against the sight

bricks and sticks and diamonds witness
a life of death is the death of life

14

Prayer

lighten up

why is Your hand
so heavy
on just poor
me?

Answer

this is the stuff
I made the heroes
out of
all the saints
and prophets and things
had to come by
this

HEROES

15

Africa

home
oh
home
the soul of your
variety
all of my bones
remember

16

i am high on the man called crazy
who has turned nigger into prince
and broken his words on every ear.
he is blinded by the truth.
his nose is sharp with courage.
this crazy man has given his own teeth
to eat devils and out of mine
he has bitten sons.

17

Earth

here is where it was dry
when it rained
and also
here
under the same
what was called
tree
it bore varicolored
flowers   children   bees
all this used to be a
place once   all this
was a nice place
once

18

for the bird who flew against our
window one morning and broke his
natural neck

my window
is his wall.
in a crash of
birdpride
he breaks the arrogance
of my definitions
and leaves me grounded
in his suicide.

19

God Send Easter

and we will lace the
jungle on
and step out
brilliant as birds
against the concrete country
feathers waving as we
dance toward jesus
sun reflecting mango
and apple as we
glory in our skin

20

so close
they come so close
to being beautiful
if they had hung on
maybe five more years
we would have been together
for these new things
and for them old niggers
to have come so close   oh
seem like some black people
missed out even more than
all the time

21

*Wise: having the ability to perceive and
    adopt the best means for accomplishing an end.*

all the best minds
come into wisdom early.
nothing anybody can say
is profound as
no money   no wine.
all the wise men
on the corner.

22

Malcolm

nobody mentioned war
but doors were closed
black women shaved their heads
black men rustled in the alleys like leaves
prophets were ambushed as they spoke
and from their holes black eagles flew
screaming through the streets

23

Eldridge

the edge
of this
Cleaver
this
 straight
sharp
single-
handled
Man
will not
rust
break, or
be broken

24

to Bobby Seale

feel free.
like my daddy
always said
jail wasn't made
for dogs,
was made for
men

25

for her hiding place
in whiteness
for Angela
straightening her hair
to cloud white eyes
for the yellow skin
of Angela
and the scholarships
to hide in
for Angela
for Angela
if we forget our sister
while they have her
let our hair fall
straight on to our backs
like death

26

Richard Penniman
when his Mama and Daddy died
put on an apron and long pants
and raised up twelve brothers and sisters.
When a whitey asked one of his brothers one time
is Little Richard a man (or what?)
he replied in perfect understanding
you bet your faggot ass
he is
you bet your dying ass.

27

Daddy
12/02 - 5/69

the days have kept on coming,
Daddy or not.   the cracks
in the sidewalk turn green
and the Indian women sell pussywillows
on the corner.   nothing remembers.
everything remembers.
in the days where Daddy was
there is a space.

my Daddy died as he lived,
a confident man.
"I'll go to Heaven," he said,
"Jesus knows me."
when his leg died, he cut it off.
"It's gone," he said, "it's gone
but I'm still here."

what will happen to the days
without you
my baby whispers to me.
the days have kept on coming
and Daddy's gone.
He knew.
He must have known and
I comfort my son with the hope
the life in the confident man.

28

poem for my sisters

like he always said
      the things of Daddy
      will find him
      leg to leg and
      lung to lung
      and the man who
      killed the bear
      so we could cross the mountain
      will cross it whole
      and holy
"all goodby ain't gone"

29

the kind of man he is
            for fred

the look of him
the beauty of the man
is in his comings and
his goings from

something is black
in all his instances

he fills
his wife with children and
with things she never knew
so that the sound of him
comes out of her in all directions

his place
is never taken

he is a dark
presence with his friends
and with his enemies
always

which is the thing
which is
the kind of man he is

SOME JESUS

30

Adam and Eve

the names
of the Things
bloom in my mouth

my body opens
into brothers

31

Cain

the land of Nod
is a desert
on my head   I
plant tears
every morning,
my brother
don't rise up

32

Moses

i walk on bones
snakes twisting
in my hand
locusts breaking my mouth
an old man
leaving slavery.
home is burning in me
like a bush
God got his eye on.

33

Solomon

I bless the black
skin of the woman
and the black
night turning around her
like a star's bed
and the black
sound of Delilah
across his prayers
for they have made me
wise

3 4

Job

Job easy
is the pride
of God

Job hard
the pride
of Job

i come to rags
like a good baby
to breakfast

3 5

Daniel

I have learned
some few things,
like when a man
walk manly
he don't stumble
even in the lion's den.

36

Jonah

What I remember
is green
in the trees
and the leaves
and the smell of mango
and yams
and if I had a drum
I would send to the brothers
—Be care full of the ocean—

3 7

John

somebody coming in blackness
like a star
and the world be a great bush
on his head
and his eyes be fire
in the city
and his mouth be true as time

he be calling the people brother
even in the prison
even in the jail

i'm just only a baptist preacher
somebody bigger than me coming
in blackness like a star

38

Mary

this kiss
as soft as cotton

over my breasts
all shiny bright

something is in this night
oh Lord have mercy on me

i feel a garden
in my mouth

between my legs
i see a tree

39

Joseph

something about this boy
has spelled my tongue
so even when my fingers tremble
on Mary
my mouth cries only
Jesus   Jesus   Jesus

40

The Calling of the Disciples

some Jesus
has come on me

I throw down my nets
into water he walks

i loose the fish
he feeds to cities

and everybody calls me
an old name

as i follow out
laughing like God's fool
behind this Jesus

41

The Raising of Lazarus

the dead shall rise again.
whoever say
dust must be dust,
don't see the trees
smell rain
remember Africa.
everything that goes
can come.
stand up!
even the dead shall rise.

42

Palm Sunday

so here come I
home again
and the people glad
giving thanks
glorying in the brother
laying turnips
for the mule to walk on
waving beets
and collards in the air

4 3

Good Friday

I rise up above my self
like a fish flying

Men will be gods
if they want it

44

Easter Sunday

while I was in the middle of the night
I saw red stars and black stars
pushed out of the sky by white ones
and I knew as sure as jungle
is the father of the world
I must slide down like a great dipper of stars
and lift men up

45

Spring Song

the green of Jesus
is breaking the ground
and the sweet
smell of delicious Jesus
is opening the house and
the dance of Jesus music
has hold of the air and
the world is turning
in the body of Jesus and
the future is possible

LUCILLE CLIFTON was born in Depew, New York, in 1936, and attended Howard University and Fredonia State Teachers College. She now lives in Baltimore with her husband, who is an educational consultant for the Model Cities Program, and their six children. Mrs. Clifton is the author of *Good Times,* a collection of poems, and three children's books: *Some of the Days of Everett Anderson, The Black BC's,* and *Everett Anderson's Christmas Coming.* Her work has appeared in *Black World, The Massachusetts Review,* and various other places. She participated in the YW–YMHA Poetry Center's Discovery Series for 1969, and has given readings in many colleges and universities.